SAM LOYD'S
Best Picture Puzzles

SAM LOYD

DOVER PUBLICATIONS, INC.
Mineola, New York

Bibliographical Note

This Dover edition, first published in 2005, contains a selection of puzzles from *Sam Loyd's Picture Puzzles with Answers,* originally published by Sam Loyd, Brooklyn, New York, in 1924.

International Standard Book Number: 0-486-44381-7

Manufactured in the United States of America
Dover Publications, Inc., 31 East 2nd Street, Mineola, N.Y. 11501

PREFACE

WHEN I am asked by editors and others who wish to cater to that legion of people, young and old, who are devoted to puzzle solving—"What is the most popular form of puzzle?" I unhesitatingly reply that the rebus "picture puzzle," is the "puzzle of the populace," as it were.

Where hundreds are partial to puzzles of the mathematical and mechanical sort or to word puzzling with charades, word-squares, anagrams, conundrums, enigmas, transpositions, etc., etc.; thousands, yes, tens of thousands, are followers of the "picture puzzle." This puzzle may be described as a word or name, represented pictorially by any sort of object, peculiar arrangement of letters, numerals, etc., the spelling or pronunciation of which is similar to that of itself.

Fifty thousand people recently participated in one of my solving contests, and the puzzles that inspired this mammoth tournament of wits were of the "picture puzzle" variety, such as compose the pages of this book. A newspaper which published one of the contests received a number of replies equal to one-third of its circulation. All of which is convincing proof of the pre-eminent popularity of the "picture puzzle."

When I say that the "picture puzzle" is the puzzle of the masses, I do not wish to be understood as classifying it as of "common, or garden variety," calling for inferior calibre of intellect. True, it engages the naturally alert faculties, rather than the scholastic and scientific. At the same time, there are qualities of wit, humor and imagination exhibited in rebus solving that betoken mental radiations of the brightest rays. I have seen a college professor strain and fail for the answer to a rebus that was solved rather readily by a bright child. It proves at least, that in some mental processes the native, unskilled wit will outstrip the polished intellect of the scholar.

We must not assume that the solving of any sort of puzzle, whether it be the cracking of a riddle or the analysis of a problem in higher mathematics, is arrived at by chance or slipshod methods. A solution is gained by reasoning along straight lines; by ingenuity and cleverness; for puzzles are not solved by dullards.

There is no better mental training than puzzle solving, and the pastime must be considered more seriously than a mere fad or amusement. I firmly believe that puzzles constitute one of the greatest educational agencies in existence, and I have always treated them from this standpoint. Parents cannot too early encourage their children's love for puzzles. Mastering a problem through the force of his own reasoning power will imbue a child with pride and self-reliance that act like a tonic on his intellectual growth.

The brightest man of my acquaintance is the manager of a newspaper, who, plucked from school at thirteen years of age, frankly attributes the splendidly trained mind he now possesses to his passionate devotion to puzzles, which set in after his formal schooling. He has the quickest head for figures I have ever encountered, and his brilliant reasoning powers are along the direct and original lines of the puzzle solver.

The peculiar fascination that lies in puzzle solving is no enigma. Human nature is inquisitive, and will spare no effort in probing for the solution of a mystery. Every thinking person experiences keen satisfaction when a perplexing puzzle has been mastered. "Eureka! I met the puzzle and the answer is mine." A puzzle is an impish challenge to our wits—"Let's see you guess me." "You bet I will;" and the tussle is on. There we have full explanation of the charm that this ancient pastime holds for most of us.

In working out the puzzles in the following pages, reference to geography, history, English, zoology, and other sources of book information is constant; and thus educational and instructive as well as entertaining. The exercise is of inestimable value to the young folks, who are unconsciously storing up useful knowledge while pursuing their labor of love.

Answers to all of the puzzles are contained in the back pages of the book, but it is to be hoped that this information will not be prematurely sought. Don't look up the answer until you have worked out what you consider must be the correct solution.

SAM LOYD.

Brooklyn, N. Y.

REBUS BOYS

The familiar first names of four boys are represented by the sketches. It is more than likely that these fellows are among your friends.

PUZZLING CHEESES

Each of the pictures suggests the name of a well-known kind of cheese. Two are of imported varieties, and the other two grandma knows how to make.

PUZZLES FROM THE ZOO

Four wild quadrupeds are represented in this group of rebus sketches. One is a great favorite at the menagerie and another is a mean and skulking fellow.

ARBOREAL REBUSES

The puzzle artist, strolling through the park with his sketch book, found four trees that are here transplanted in the rebus garden.

JUICY PUZZLES

Four kinds of luscious fruit are here pictured in rebus form. Two of them grow on trees, another on a vine and the fourth on a bush.

A PUZZLING TICKER

The inside of a watch is a puzzle to most of us, but the names of its principal parts are well known. Each rebus represents one of those parts.

6

A CHRISTMAS ZOO

A little zoologist's Christmas list will make his tree look like our sketch if all his wishes for animal toys come true. How many creatures can you find?

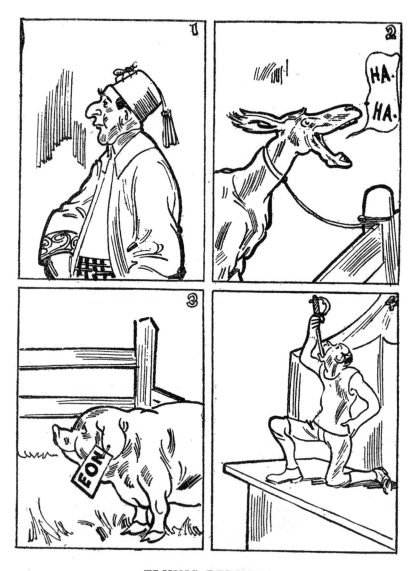

FLYING REBUSES

Each sketch represents the name of a bird. The dictionary says that one of them is a large Australian insectivorous kingfisher.

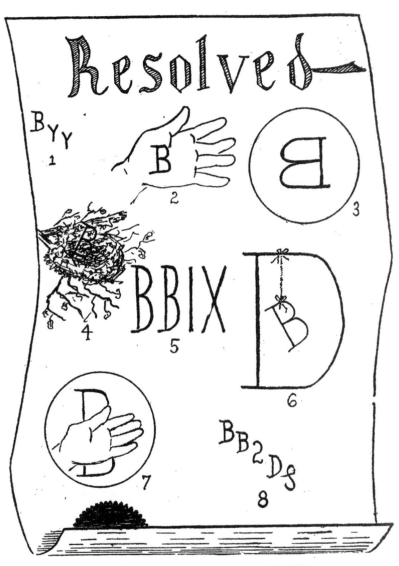

NEW YEAR'S RESOLUTIONS

Here are eight rebus resolutions for the New Year that, if carried out, will make a fellow's conduct about ninety-nine per cent perfect.

FLORAL REBUSES

In this rebus garden you are invited to pluck the names of four flowers. Even if you are not up in horticulture you have often heard of these blossoms.

A PUZZLING GOOD BOY

Of the many fine qualities to look for in a manly boy here are four of his best points translated into rebus form.

CRAWLING PUZZLES

The names of four insects of well-known species are here presented in rebus form. Three of them you will probably guess off-hand but the other is hard to catch.

PUZZLING ANATOMY

The class in physiology will now come to attention, so that we may see who can discover the four parts of the human body represented by the sketches.

PUZZLING PRESIDENTS

The surnames of four ex-Presidents of the United States are represented by these pictures. This is a good time to read over the full list.

STATES AND COUNTRIES

What four states and countries do these pictures represent? One is of a nation that played a most heroic part in the World War I.

REBUS VEHICLES

Each picture represents the name of an old-fashioned horse-drawn vehicle. Granddad will help you out with these if you are too modern.

PASTRY PUZZLES

Each of the rebuses represents a sort of cake with which we are all familiar. They will make your mouth water after you guess them.

THE EMPIRE STATE

Each of the sketches represents a city, town or village in the State of New York. In scanning the map don't fail to take in Long Island.

CONFECTIONERY PUZZLES

Four sorts of popular candy are to be found in these pictures. Two are of the old-fashioned kind, and the other two more up to date.

THE ARTIST'S PUZZLES

"Why shouldn't my palette provide some good puzzle material?" said the artist. And so it did, for each of the sketches represents a color I found there.

RANKING OFFICERS

In a photograph taken during a famous Frenchman's visit to West Point appears four officers of different ranks. Those four commissions are here represented.

IN A LADY'S HANDBAG

The three little rebuses represent articles that one would be almost sure to find in the average woman's handbag. What are they?

IN A BOY'S POCKET

As Johnny's teacher emptied his pockets several articles came to view that furnish good puzzle material. Each picture represents one of Johnny's treasures.

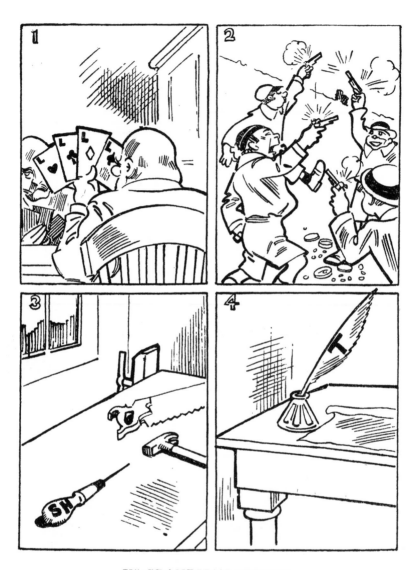

IN GRANDMA'S TRUNK

On a rainy day the children invaded the garret and rummaged through Grandma's trunk. Each of the pictures represents something that was brought to view.

PUZZLES ON FOOT

Footwear furnishes the subject for this page, so we are expected to find in each of the little pictures the name of a familiar footcovering.

SPICY PUZZLES

This page of rebuses might be called highly flavored, for each of the four represents a well-known spice with a snappy flavor.

PUZZLING COIFFURES

Four young ladies issued from the hair-dresser's studio, and the four styles in which their locks were arranged are set forth in the sketches.

LIVING-ROOM PUZZLES

Each of the four pictures, in a rebus way, stands for something that we are sure to encounter in the living-room of a comfortable home.

MASSACHUSETTS TOWNS

In a tour of the Bay State we passed through four places whose names provided subjects for this group of rebus sketches. Can you guess them?

DECLARATION FATHERS

Each of the sketches represents the surname of a signer of the Declaration of Independence. Now we shall have to get out our history books.

AMERICAN INDIANS

Each sketch represents the name of a well-known tribe of American Indians. Let us see if can you name them all.

SCHOOL DAYS

Four school studies that boys and girls will all have to wrestle with, if they are not already so engaged, can be found in these four pictures.

WEAPONS OF WAR

Let us hope that the nations will never again take up against one another such weapons as are here represented—for then there would be no more wars.

BEANS A LA REBUS

The humble bean, in its various forms, provides good puzzle diet, so let us see who can discover the four species here served in rebus form.

PUZZLE GEMS

Each of the sketches represents the name of a precious stone that one is likely to see in any high-class jeweler's window; and perhaps you possess all four of them.

OUTDOOR SPORTS

Each of the sketches represents the name of a well-known outdoor game. Even if you are not of the athletic type you have often heard of these four sports.

DRESS-GOODS PUZZLES

When mother was getting the girls' dresses ready for vacation days, she used four sorts of material that are here presented in rebus form.

PUZZLING VEGETABLES

Each of the pictures represents the name of a vegetable of the "common, or garden variety." Two are of the same family.

PUZZLING INSECTS

Strolling about the country in vacation days, you are almost sure to encounter all four sorts of insects represented by these pictures. Can you name them?

PUZZLING GIRLS

We selected a group of little girls to pose for this page. Each of the pictures represents a very pretty feminine first name.

CIVIL WAR GENERALS

Each of the four sketches represents in a rebus way the surname of a distinguished General who fought for the Blue or the Gray.

HEADY PUZZLES

Each of the pictures represents some feature to be found on or in one's head. That, of course, includes the face, or any part above the neck.

REBUS BOYS

The first names of four boys are here presented in rebus form. They're good, democratic names, without flourish.

SHIP AHOY PUZZLES

Each of the pictures represents some sort of craft, large or small, that man has fashioned for navigating the waters. You have heard of them all.

AT THE DRY GOODS SHOP

When mother returned from her shopping tour, the children found in her parcels the four articles here depicted in rebus dress.

THANKSGIVING DINNER

Each of the sketches represents something especially appropriate for the Thanksgiving dinner. The four together would make a satisfactory repast.

PUZZLING CANINES

The names of four familiar breeds of dogs are represented by the pictures. They are not of the fashionable world, but are of the staunch and useful types.

PUZZLING FRUIT

Each of the four sketches suggests the name of a luscious fruit. Three are fairly easy to guess, but the fourth will stump the average puzzler.

PUZZLING ORCHESTRA

Each of the pictures represents the name of a well-known musical instrument. To play upon two of them requires good lung power.

AN ANIMAL HUNT

Each of the pictures represents the name of some wild animal. It is more than likely that all four are boarding at the nearest Zoo.

MARKET BASKET PUZZLES

When the good wife opened her market basket the first four things that came to view provided subjects for these rebus sketches. What are they?

PUZZLES FROM THE WOODS

Each of the sketches represents the name of a familiar tree. The four are natives of North America and are frequently seen growing together.

REBUSES IN BLOOM

Here is a rebus nosegay, composed of four beautiful flowers. How many of the buds can you pluck?

ANSWERS TO THE PICTURE PUZZLES

Corresponding to the Numbered Pages

Page

1. REBUS BOYS—
    1. Isaac. 2. Paul. 3. Oscar. 4. Roland.

2. PUZZLING CHEESES—
    1. Edam. 2. Roquefort. 3. Cream. 4. Pot-cheese.

3. PUZZLES FROM THE ZOO—
    1. Eland. 2. Elephant. 3. Hyena. 4. Tapir.

4. ARBOREAL REBUSES—
    1. Dogwood. 2. Rubber. 3. Ash. 4. Palm.

5. JUICY PUZZLES—
    1. Alligator Pear. 2. Grapes. 3. Cherries. 4. Currants.

6. A PUZZLING TICKER—
    1. Hairspring. 2. Minute hand. 3. Dial. 4. Wheels.

7. A CHRISTMAS ZOO—
    Cat, Squirrel, Parrot, Giraffe, Armadillo, Anteater, Croco-
    dile, Tortoise, Zebu, Toucan, Deer, Seal, Ape, Penguin,
    Porcupine, Dachshund, Camel, Hyena, Bear, Elephant,
    Owl, Hippopotamus, Eagle, Rhinoceros, Lion, Cow, Leo-
    pard, Kangaroo, Sloth, Ostrich, Zebra, Tiger, Rabbit,
    Buffalo, Horse, Goat, Pig—37.

8. FLYING REBUSES—
    1. Pheasant. 2. Laughing jackass. 3. Pigeon. 4. Swallow.

9. NEW YEAR'S RESOLUTIONS—
    1. Be wise. 2. Be on hand. 3. Be backward in nothing.
    4. Be honest. 5. Be benign. 6. Be independent. 7. Be
    behindhand in naught. 8. Be studious.

10. FLORAL REBUSES—
    1. Dandelion. 2. Foxglove. 3. Orchid. 4. Lady's Slipper.

ANSWERS TO THE PICTURE PUZZLES

11. A PUZZLING GOOD BOY—
    1. Honesty (on ST). 2. Common sense (cents).
    3. Courage (cur age). 4. Uprightness.

12. CRAWLING PUZZLES—
    1. Caterpillar. 2. Beetle. 3. Darning Needle. 4. Scorpion.

13. PUZZLING ANATOMY—
    1. Arms. 2. Chest. 3. Veins. 4. Two feet.

14. PUZZLING PRESIDENTS—
    1. Washington. 2. Taylor. 3. Adams. 4. Garfield.

15. STATES AND COUNTRIES—
    1. Belgium. 2. Wales. 3. Cuba. 4. Tennessee.

16. REBUS VEHICLES—
    1. Cart. 2. Hack. 3. Sulky. 4. Shay.

17. PASTRY PUZZLES—
    1. Lady Fingers. 2. Marble (cake). 3. Citron (sit run).
    4. Pound (cake).

18. THE EMPIRE STATE—
    1. Buffalo. 2. Catskill. 3. Cohoes. 4. Sea Cliff.

19. CONFECTIONERY PUZZLES—
    1. Kisses. 2. Butter Scotch. 3. Bon Bons. 4. Molasses
    Candy.

20. THE ARTIST'S PUZZLES—
    1. Yellow. 2. Blue. 3. Pink. 4. Red (read).

21. RANKING OFFICERS—
    1. Captain. 2. Marshal. 3. Lieutenant (loot ten ant).
    4. Colonel.

22. IN A LADY'S HANDBAG—
    1. Pins. 2. Receipts. 3. Bills.

23. IN A BOY'S POCKET—
    1. Top. 2. Marbles. 3. String. 4. Pennies.

ANSWERS TO THE PICTURE PUZZLES

24. IN GRANDMA'S TRUNK—
    1. Laces. 2. Caps. 3. Shawl. 4. Quilt.

25. PUZZLES ON FOOT—
    1. Slippers. 2. Shoes. 3. Pumps. 4. Sandals.

26. SPICY PUZZLES—
    1. Capers. 2. Ginger. 3. Cloves. 4. Allspice.

27. PUZZLING COIFFURES—
    1. Bobbed. 2. Bangs. 3. Curled. 4. Waves.

28. LIVING-ROOM PUZZLES—
    1. Lamp. 2. Cabinet. 3. Easy chair. 4. Couch.

29. MASSACHUSETTS TOWNS—
    1. Concord. 2. Gardner 3. Hyannis. 4. Manchester.

30. DECLARATION FATHERS—
    1. Clymer. 2. Chase. 3. Paine. 4. Smith.

31. AN INDIAN HUNT—
    1. Crow. 2. Blackfoot. 3. Apache. 4. Pawnee.

32. SCHOOL DAYS—
    1. Reading. 2. English. 3. Penmanship. 4. Mathematics.

33. WEAPONS OF WAR—
    1. Bayonet. 2. Cannon. 3. Mortar. 4. Revolver.

34. BEANS A LA REBUS—
    1. Kidney. 2. Lima. 3. String. 4. Wax.

35. PUZZLE GEMS—
    1. Diamond. 2. Pearl. 3. Beryl. 4. Ruby.

36. OUTDOOR SPORTS—
    1. Lacrosse. 2. Lawn tennis. 3. Golf. 4. Football.

37. DRESS-GOODS PUZZLES—
    1. Satin. 2. Muslin. 3. Cotton. 4. Linen.

38. PUZZLING VEGETABLES—
    1. Spinach. 2. Beans. 3. Cauliflower. 4. Cabbage.

ANSWERS TO THE PICTURE PUZZLES

Page

39. PUZZLING INSECTS—
1. Butterflies. 2. Dragonflies. 3. Hornet. 4. Red ants.

40. PUZZLING GIRLS—
1. Rose. 2. Dora. 3. Pansy. 4. Mary (mare E).

41. CIVIL WAR GENERALS—
1. Grant. 2. Hood. 3. Butler. 4. Wheeler.

42. HEADY PUZZLES—
1. Lash. 2. Palate. 3. Pupils. 4. Temple.

43. REBUS BOYS—
1. Henry. 2. Carl. 3. Peter (pea eater). 4. James.

44. SHIP AHOY PUZZLES—
1. Cutter. 2. Ark. 3. Bark. 4. Yawl.

45. AT THE DRY GOODS SHOP—
1. Aprons. 2. Needles (need L's). 3. Braid. 4. Hose.

46. THANKSGIVING DINNER—
1. Celery. 2. Mince pie. 3. Turkey. 4. Cranberries.

47. PUZZLING CANINES—
1. Pointer. 2. Pug. 3. Great Dane. 4. Bull.

48. PUZZLING FRUIT—
1. Blackberries. 2. Peaches (P chess). 3. Pears. 4. Dates.

49. PUZZLING ORCHESTRA—
1. Cornet. 2. Lyre. 3. Cymbals (symbols). 4. Bugle.

50. AN ANIMAL HUNT—
1. Groundhog. 2. Weasel. 3. Monkey. 4. Mongoose.

51. MARKET BASKET PUZZLES—
1. Starch. 2. Ceylon tea. 3. Thyme. 4. Molasses.

52. PUZZLES FROM THE WOODS—
1. Pine. 2. Maple. 3. Fir. 4. Spruce.

53. REBUSES IN BLOOM—
1. Peony (P on knee). 2. Tulip (tool IP). 3. Sweet peas. 4. Dog rose.